What the
BIBLE
Says
about

PRAYING

What the
BIBLE
Says
about
PRAYING

BARBOUR
PUBLISHING

Scripture quotations marked NIV are taken from the HOLY BIBLE, NEW INTERNATIONAL VERSION®. NIV®. Copyright © 1973, 1978, 1984 by International Bible Society. Used by permission of Zondervan. All rights reserved.

Scripture quotations marked NASB are taken from the NEW AMERICAN STANDARD BIBLE, © 1960, 1962, 1963, 1968, 1971, 1972, 1973, 1975, 1977, 1995 by The Lockman Foundation. Used by permission.

Scripture quotations marked NCV are taken from the NEW CENTURY VERSION®. Copyright © 2005 by Thomas Nelson, Inc. Used by permission. All rights reserved.

Scripture quotations marked NLT are taken from the *Holy Bible*, New Living Translation, copyright © 1996, 2004. Used by permission of Tyndale House Publishers, Inc. Wheaton, Illinois 60189, U.S.A. All rights reserved.

Scripture quotations marked CEV are from the Contemporary English Version, Copyright © 1991, 1992, 1995 by the American Bible Society. Used by permission.

Scripture quotations marked NKJV are taken from the New King James Version®. Copyright © 1982 by Thomas Nelson, Inc. Used by permission. All rights reserved.

Scripture quotations marked MSG are from *THE MESSAGE*. Copyright © by Eugene H. Peterson 1993, 1994, 1995, 1996, 2000, 2001, 2002. Used by permission of NavPress Publishing Group.

Scripture quotations marked ESV are from The Holy Bible, English Standard Version®, copyright © 2001 by Crossway Bibles, a publishing ministry of Good News Publishers. Used by permission. All rights reserved.

Scripture quotations marked KJV are taken from the King James Version of the Bible.

Published by Barbour Publishing, Inc., P.O. Box 719, Uhrichsville, Ohio 44683, www.barbourbooks.com

Our mission is to publish and distribute inspirational products offering exceptional value and biblical encouragement to the masses.

Member of the
Evangelical Christian
Publishers Association

Printed in the United States of America

CONTENTS

INTRODUCTION

DRAWING NEAR

Some people pray while they kneel. Others pray as they walk. Some people get up early to spend lengthy times in prayer, whereas others lie in bed and whisper a few words of prayer before drifting off to sleep.

Though people pray in many different ways, there are few who feel their prayer lives need no improvement. Most of us want to experience genuine intimacy in our relationship with God, yet this often seems elusive or difficult to achieve. We either struggle with understanding what it means to draw near to God, or we wrestle with practicing it.

It probably comes as no surprise that the Bible has much to say on the topic of prayer. Explore the following pages to discover the Bible's instructions for prayer—and to see how the men and women of the Bible drew near to God.

CHAPTER 1

THE VALUE OF PRAYER

One of the best practices I've employed in my prayer life is to take it slow. By nature, I simply want to get my prayers done, check the task off my list, and get on with parts of my day that feel more productive. A number of years ago, though, I found the value of taking my time in prayer. Now I often linger until I can fully clear my mind of distraction and truly connect with God. I can't always afford to take that time every day, but I try to do so at least once or twice a week.

■ Claire, age 27, Ireland ■

REMAINING IN GOD'S PRESENCE

◾ Better is one day in your courts than a
thousand elsewhere; I would rather be a
doorkeeper in the house of my God than
dwell in the tents of the wicked.

PSALM 84:10 NIV

◾ You know me inside and out, you hold me
together, you never fail to stand me tall in
your presence so I can look you in the eye.

PSALM 41:12 MSG

◾ Seek the LORD while He may be found;
Call upon Him while He is near.

ISAIAH 55:6 NASB

◾ May the grace of the Lord Jesus Christ, and
the love of God, and the fellowship of the
Holy Spirit be with you all.

2 CORINTHIANS 13:14 NIV

■ Each day the LORD pours his unfailing love upon me, and through each night I sing his songs, praying to God who gives me life.

PSALM 42:8 NLT

■ When we trust in him, we're free to say whatever needs to be said, bold to go wherever we need to go.

EPHESIANS 3:12 MSG

■ He found them in a desert land,
    in an empty, howling wasteland.
He surrounded them and watched over
    them; he guarded them as he would
    guard his own eyes.

DEUTERONOMY 32:10 NLT

REMINDING YOURSELF OF GOD'S CARE

The LORD is near to all who call on him,
to all who call on him in truth.

PSALM 145:18 NIV

GOD keeps an eye on his friends,
his ears pick up every moan and groan.

PSALM 34:15 MSG

You don't need to cry anymore. The Lord is
kind, and as soon as he hears your cries for
help, he will come.

ISAIAH 30:19 CEV

I pray that you, being rooted and established
in love, may have power, together with all the
saints, to grasp how wide and long and high
and deep is the love of Christ, and to know
this love that surpasses knowledge—that you
may be filled to the measure of all the full-
ness of God.

EPHESIANS 3:17–19 NIV

STRENGTHENING YOUR SPIRITUAL LIFE

■ But you, dear friends, carefully build yourselves up in this most holy faith by praying
in the Holy Spirit.

JUDE 20 MSG

■ Call to me and I will answer you and tell you
great and unsearchable things you do not
know.

JEREMIAH 33:3 NIV

■ Therefore, I urge you, brothers, in view of
God's mercy, to offer your bodies as living
sacrifices, holy and pleasing to God—this is
your spiritual act of worship. Do not conform
any longer to the pattern of this world, but
be transformed by the renewing of your
mind. Then you will be able to test and approve what God's will is—his good, pleasing
and perfect will.

ROMANS 12:1–2 NIV

■ Immediately the boy's father exclaimed, "I do believe; help me overcome my unbelief!"

MARK 9:24 NIV

■ Moses said to the LORD, "You have been telling me, 'Lead these people,' but you have not let me know whom you will send with me. You have said, 'I know you by name and you have found favor with me.' If you are pleased with me, teach me your ways so I may know you and continue to find favor with you. Remember that this nation is your people."

EXODUS 33:12–13 NIV

EXPERIENCING THE BLESSING

■ "If you sinful people know how to give good gifts to your children, how much more will your heavenly Father give good gifts to those who ask him."

MATTHEW 7:11 NLT

■ "Until now you have not asked for anything in my name. Ask and you will receive, and your joy will be complete."

JOHN 16:24 NIV

■ For there is no difference between Jew and Gentile—the same Lord is Lord of all and richly blesses all who call on him.

ROMANS 10:12 NIV

■ You will show me the way of life, granting me the joy of your presence and the pleasures of living with you forever.

PSALM 16:11 NLT

ONE MOMENT
AT A TIME

TAKE SOME TIME

▪ **Move prayer up the priority list.** For many of us, prayer is the first thing to go when the schedule gets chaotic. When something has to be cut from your day, choose something else. Prayer is too valuable to cut it regularly from your schedule.

▪ **Commit to a prayer experiment.** Carve out time to pray for the next fourteen days no matter how you feel or how busy your schedule becomes. At the end of the two weeks, write down the ways you saw prayer make a difference in your life and attitude.

Realize it's okay to ask God for help. Some people are hesitant to ask God to bless them, but God wants to help and bless His children. Make sure your prayers include specific requests for the help you need.

CHAPTER 2

MEETING THE GOD OF OUR PRAYER

I grew up in a stuffy church where the only prayers I ever said were the memorized ones we prayed on Sunday mornings. When I went to college, I met some other Christians who surprised me by their constant encouragement to pray. I took their advice—partly because I wanted to humor them, and partly because I was hoping they were right about God. I was hoping to find a God who really did care about me and my life. I was so happy to learn that they were right! God is much bigger and more personal than I had ever understood.

■ Jaimie, age 24, Iowa ■

FINDING HIM APPROACHABLE

One thing I ask of the LORD,
> this is what I seek:
that I may dwell in the house of the LORD
> all the days of my life,
to gaze upon the beauty of the LORD
> and to seek him in his temple.

PSALM 27:4 NIV

But now in Christ Jesus you who once were far off have been brought near by the blood of Christ.

EPHESIANS 2:13 NKJV

And he came and preached peace to you who were far off and peace to those who were near. For through him we both have access in one Spirit to the Father.

EPHESIANS 2:17–18 ESV

■ Blessed are those you choose and bring
near to live in your courts!
We are filled with the good things of your
house, of your holy temple.

PSALM 65:4 NIV

■ Come near to God, and he will come near
to you. Clean up your lives, you sinners. Purify
your hearts, you people who can't make up
your mind.

JAMES 4:8 CEV

■ The Spirit and the bride say, "Come!" And
let him who hears say, "Come!" Whoever is
thirsty, let him come; and whoever wishes,
let him take the free gift of the water of life.

REVELATION 22:17 NIV

23

"The God who made the world and everything in it is the Lord of heaven and earth and does not live in temples built by hands. And he is not served by human hands, as if he needed anything, because he himself gives all men life and breath and everything else. From one man he made every nation of men, that they should inhabit the whole earth; and he determined the times set for them and the exact places where they should live. God did this so that men would seek him and perhaps reach out for him and find him, though he is not far from each one of us."

ACTS 17:24–27 NIV

LEARNING HE IS PERSONAL

■ GOD, high above, sees far below;
no matter the distance, he knows everything
about us.

PSALM 138:6 MSG

■ Taste and see that the LORD is good;
blessed is the man who takes refuge in him.

PSALM 34:8 NIV

■ "And Solomon, my son, learn to know the
God of your ancestors intimately. Worship
and serve him with your whole heart and a
willing mind. For the LORD sees every heart
and knows every plan and thought. If you
seek him, you will find him. But if you forsake
him, he will reject you forever."

1 CHRONICLES 28:9 NLT

■ Therefore, since we have been justified through faith, we have peace with God through our Lord Jesus Christ.

ROMANS 5:1 NIV

■ "Let us acknowledge the LORD; let us press on to acknowledge him. As surely as the sun rises, he will appear; he will come to us like the winter rains, like the spring rains that water the earth."

HOSEA 6:3 NIV

■ But the foundation that God has laid is solid. On it is written, "The Lord knows who his people are. So everyone who worships the Lord must turn away from evil."

2 TIMOTHY 2:19 CEV

■ "Two sparrows cost only a penny, but not even one of them can die without your Father's knowing it. God even knows how many hairs are on your head. So don't be afraid. You are worth much more than many sparrows."

MATTHEW 10:29–31 NCV

KNOWING THAT HE HEARS

■ LORD, you hear the desire of the afflicted;
you will strengthen their heart; you will incline
your ear.

PSALM 10:17 ESV

■ He who planted the ear, does he not hear?
He who formed the eye, does he not see?

PSALM 94:9 ESV

■ Listen! The LORD's arm is not too weak to
save you, nor is his ear too deaf to hear
you call.

ISAIAH 59:1 NLT

■ In my alarm I said,
"I am cut off from your sight!"
Yet you heard my cry for mercy
when I called to you for help.

PSALM 31:22 NIV

■ Listen to my cry for help, my King and my
God, for I pray to no one but you.

PSALM 5:2 NLT

■ I call on you, O God, for you will answer me;
give ear to me and hear my prayer.

PSALM 17:6 NIV

■ For the eyes of the Lord are on the righteous
and his ears are attentive to their prayer,
but the face of the Lord is against those who
do evil.

1 PETER 3:12 NIV

■ He grants the desires of those who fear him;
he hears their cries for help and rescues
them.

PSALM 145:19 NLT

■ For the LORD hears the cries of the needy;
he does not despise his imprisoned people.

PSALM 69:33 NLT

■ The LORD has heard my plea;
the LORD will answer my prayer.

PSALM 6:9 NLT

■ "Then you will call upon me and come and
pray to me, and I will listen to you."

JEREMIAH 29:12 NIV

■ The LORD said: I have seen how my people
are suffering as slaves in Egypt, and I have
heard them beg for my help because of the
way they are being mistreated. I feel sorry for
them, and I have come down to rescue them
from the Egyptians.

EXODUS 3:7–8 CEV

■ But certainly God has heard me; He has
attended to the voice of my prayer.
Blessed be God, who has not turned
away my prayer,
nor His mercy from me!

PSALM 66:19–20 NKJV

■ But you, O God, do see trouble and grief;
    you consider it to take it in hand.
The victim commits himself to you;
    you are the helper of the fatherless.

PSALM 10:14 NIV

■ This is the confidence which we have before
Him, that, if we ask anything according to His
will, He hears us.

1 JOHN 5:14 NASB

■ I called on your name, O LORD,
    from the depths of the pit.
You heard my plea: "Do not close your ears
    to my cry for relief."
You came near when I called you,
    and you said, "Do not fear."
O Lord, you took up my case;
    you redeemed my life.

LAMENTATIONS 3:55–58 NIV

■ Praise be to the LORD, for he has heard my
cry for mercy.

PSALM 28:6 NIV

TRUSTING HIM TO ANSWER

▪ Everyone will come to you because you answer prayer.

PSALM 65:2 CEV

▪ "So I say to you: Ask and it will be given to you; seek and you will find; knock and the door will be opened to you. For everyone who asks receives; he who seeks finds; and to him who knocks, the door will be opened."

LUKE 11:9–10 NIV

▪ "Whatever you ask in my name, this I will do, that the Father may be glorified in the Son. If you ask me anything in my name, I will do it."

JOHN 14:13–14 ESV

▪ "You didn't choose me. I chose you. I appointed you to go and produce lasting fruit, so that the Father will give you whatever you ask for, using my name."

JOHN 15:16 NLT

31

■ They caused the cry of the poor to come to him, and he heard the cry of the afflicted.

JOB 34:28 ESV

■ Then my enemies will turn back when
    I call for help.
By this I will know that God is for me.

PSALM 56:9 NIV

■ And if we know that he hears us—whatever we ask—we know that we have what we asked of him.

1 JOHN 5:15 NIV

■ The LORD says, "I will rescue those who love me. I will protect those who trust in my name."

PSALM 91:14 NLT

■ "Therefore I tell you, whatever you ask for in prayer, believe that you have received it, and it will be yours."

MARK 11:24 NIV

He will respond to the prayer of the destitute; he will not despise their plea.

PSALM 102:17 NIV

Elijah was just as human as we are, and for three and a half years his prayers kept the rain from falling. But when he did pray for rain, it fell from the skies and made the crops grow.

JAMES 5:17–18 CEV

About that time Hezekiah became deathly ill. He prayed to the LORD, who healed him and gave him a miraculous sign.

2 CHRONICLES 32:24 NLT

"And whatever things you ask in prayer, believing, you will receive."

MATTHEW 21:22 NKJV

■ Then you will call, and the LORD will answer;
    you will cry for help, and he will say:
Here am I.

ISAIAH 58:9 NIV

■ Tears of joy will stream down their faces,
    and I will lead them home with
        great care.
They will walk beside quiet streams
    and on smooth paths where they will
        not stumble.
For I am Israel's father,
    and Ephraim is my oldest child.

JEREMIAH 31:9 NLT

■ "As soon as you began to pray, an answer
was given, which I have come to tell you, for
you are highly esteemed. Therefore, consider
the message and understand the vision."

DANIEL 9:23 NIV

■ He said to them, "Because of your little faith. For truly, I say to you, if you have faith like a grain of mustard seed, you will say to this mountain, 'Move from here to there,' and it will move, and nothing will be impossible for you."

MATTHEW 17:20 ESV

ONE MOMENT
AT A TIME

GETTING
COMFORTABLE

Explore a new routine. If you've always prayed kneeling, try standing up or going for a walk. If you've always prayed in the evening, try getting up and making prayer a part of your morning. By doing so, you may be able to make prayer less rote and more personal.

Focus on God. People are often surprised to learn that God is personal and cares for them and their needs. God knows everything about you, and He went to great lengths to make it possible for you to know Him also. Before you pray next, read a Psalm or two from the Bible and find an attribute or name of God that strikes you afresh. As you pray, reflect on how that attribute can affect the praise and requests you bring before Him.

Bring a blank "to do" list. As much as possible, try to pray in an environment that is conducive to uninterrupted thought. If you become distracted and begin thinking about tasks you need to complete, then have a paper and pen nearby so you can write down the items on your mind and get back to the business of prayer.

CHAPTER 3

THE PRAYER OF ADORATION

The longer I spend praising God, the more I'm reminded that life is much bigger than me and the concerns I have for my family. As I praise Him, I'm reminded of how wide, deep, and tall He is, and then the problems of the day seem to get put into better perspective. And while I still worry about my daughter and her kids, praising God reminds me that the almighty God of the universe is still in charge, still sees the big picture, and still cares about me (and them) very much!

■ Millie, age 66, Vermont ■

UNDERSTANDING OUR
DUTY TO PRAISE

■ But you are a chosen people, a royal priest-
hood, a holy nation, a people belonging to
God, that you may declare the praises of
him who called you out of darkness into his
wonderful light.

1 PETER 2:9 NIV

■ Then a voice came from the throne, saying:
"Praise our God, all you his servants,
  you who fear him, both small and great!"

REVELATION 19:5 NIV

■ Blessed be the LORD, the God of Israel,
From everlasting even to everlasting.
And let all the people say, "Amen."
Praise the LORD!

PSALM 106:48 NASB

Sing to the LORD, you saints of his;
praise his holy name.

PSALM 30:4 NIV

The LORD will bring about justice and praise
in every nation on earth, like flowers
blooming in a garden.

ISAIAH 61:11 CEV

Praise God, all you people of Israel;
praise the LORD, the source of Israel's life.

PSALM 68:26 NLT

"Do you hear what these children are
    saying?" they asked him.
"Yes," replied Jesus, "have you never read,
    " 'From the lips of children and infants
    you have ordained praise'?"

MATTHEW 21:16 NIV

Sing to God, O kingdoms of the earth;
Sing praises to the Lord, Selah.

PSALM 68:32 NASB

41

■ "For as a belt is bound around a man's waist, so I bound the whole house of Israel and the whole house of Judah to me," declares the LORD, "to be my people for my renown and praise and honor. But they have not listened."

JEREMIAH 13:11 NIV

■ And you also were included in Christ when you heard the word of truth, the gospel of your salvation. Having believed, you were marked in him with a seal, the promised Holy Spirit, who is a deposit guaranteeing our inheritance until the redemption of those who are God's possession—to the praise of his glory.

EPHESIANS 1:13–15 NIV

■ The wild animals honor me, the jackals and the owls, because I provide water in the desert and streams in the wasteland, to give drink to my people, my chosen.

ISAIAH 43:20 NIV

STANDING IN AWE OF GOD

▪ LORD All-Powerful, you are greater than all others. No one is like you, and you alone are God. Everything we have heard about you is true.

2 SAMUEL 7:22 CEV

▪ Join with me in praising the wonderful name of the LORD our God.

DEUTERONOMY 32:3 CEV

▪ Fear the LORD your God and serve him. Hold fast to him and take your oaths in his name. He is your praise; he is your God, who performed for you those great and awesome wonders you saw with your own eyes.

DEUTERONOMY 10:20–21 NIV

For great is the LORD and most worthy of
    praise; he is to be feared above all gods.
For all the gods of the nations are idols,
    but the LORD made the heavens.
Splendor and majesty are before him;
    strength and glory are in his sanctuary.
Ascribe to the LORD, O families of nations,
    ascribe to the LORD glory and strength.
Ascribe to the LORD the glory due his name;
    bring an offering and come into his courts.
Worship the LORD in the splendor of his
    holiness; tremble before him, all the earth.

PSALM 96:4–9 NIV

LORD, our Lord, how majestic is Your name
in all the earth, who have displayed Your
splendor above the heavens!

PSALM 8:1 NASB

"There is no one like you, O LORD, and there
is no God but you, as we have heard with
our own ears."

1 CHRONICLES 17:20 NIV

Oh, the depth of the riches of the wisdom
and knowledge of God!
How unsearchable his judgments,
and his paths beyond tracing out!
"Who has known the mind of the Lord?
Or who has been his counselor?"
"Who has ever given to God,
that God should repay him?"
For from him and through him and to him
are all things.
To him be the glory forever! Amen.

ROMANS 11:33–36 NIV

In the council of the holy ones God is greatly
feared; he is more awesome than all who
surround him.

PSALM 89:7 NIV

Lord, you have been our dwelling place in
all generations. Before the mountains were
brought forth, or ever you had formed the
earth and the world, from everlasting to
everlasting you are God.

PSALM 90:1–2 ESV

■ "Praise be to you, O Lord, God of our father Israel, from everlasting to everlasting. Yours, O Lord, is the greatness and the power and the glory and the majesty and the splendor, for everything in heaven and earth is yours. Yours, O Lord, is the kingdom; you are exalted as head over all. Wealth and honor come from you; you are the ruler of all things. In your hands are strength and power to exalt and give strength to all. Now, our God, we give you thanks, and praise your glorious name."

1 Chronicles 29:10–13 NIV

■ You turn man back into dust
　　And say, "Return, O children of men."
For a thousand years in Your sight
　　Are like yesterday when it passes by,
Or as a watch in the night.

Psalm 90:3–4 NASB

■ Come and see what God has done, how awesome his works in man's behalf!

Psalm 66:5 NIV

■ LORD, you have examined my heart
    and know everything about me.
You know when I sit down or stand up.
You know my thoughts even when I'm far away.
You see me when I travel and when I rest
    at home.
You know everything I do.
You know what I am going to say even
    before I say it, LORD.
You go before me and follow me.
You place your hand of blessing on my head.
Such knowledge is too wonderful for me,
    too great for me to understand!

PSALM 139:1–6 NLT

■ LORD, I have heard of your fame;
I stand in awe of your deeds, O LORD.
Renew them in our day,
in our time make them known;
in wrath remember mercy.

HABAKKUK 3:2 NIV

47

Let them know that you, whose name is the
LORD—that you alone are the Most High
over all the earth.

PSALM 83:18 NIV

"Who among the gods is like you, O LORD?
Who is like you—majestic in holiness,
awesome in glory, working wonders?"

EXODUS 15:11 NIV

"Declare and set forth your case;
Indeed, let them consult together
Who has announced this from of old?
Who has long since declared it?
Is it not I, the LORD?
And there is no other God besides Me,
A righteous God and a Savior;
There is none except Me.
Turn to Me and be saved, all the ends of
    the earth;
For I am God, and there is no other."

ISAIAH 45:21–22 NASB

REVERING HIM

■ Great is the LORD! He is most worthy
   of praise!
He is to be feared above all gods.

> 1 CHRONICLES 16:25 NLT

■ Therefore, since we are receiving a kingdom
that cannot be shaken, let us be thankful, and
so worship God acceptably with reverence
and awe, for our "God is a consuming fire."

> HEBREWS 12:28–29 NIV

■ "Great and marvelous are your deeds,
   Lord God Almighty.
Just and true are your ways, King of the ages.
Who will not fear you, O Lord, and bring
   glory to your name?
For you alone are holy.
All nations will come and worship before you,
   for your righteous acts have been
   revealed."

> REVELATION 15:3–4 NIV

49

■ "Stand up and bless the Lord your God from everlasting to everlasting. Blessed be your glorious name, which is exalted above all blessing and praise.

"You are the Lord, you alone. You have made heaven, the heaven of heavens, with all their host, the earth and all that is on it, the seas and all that is in them; and you preserve all of them; and the host of heaven worships you."

NEHEMIAH 9:5–6 ESV

■ How great are your works, O Lord,
    how profound your thoughts!
The senseless man does not know,
    fools do not understand, that though
    the wicked spring up like grass
    and all evildoers flourish,
    they will be forever destroyed.
But you, O Lord, are exalted forever.

PSALM 92:5–8 NIV

■ It was in the year King Uzziah died that I saw the Lord. He was sitting on a lofty throne, and the train of his robe filled the Temple. Attending him were mighty seraphim, each having six wings. With two wings they covered their faces, with two they covered their feet, and with two they flew. They were calling out to each other, "Holy, holy, holy is the LORD of Heaven's Armies! The whole earth is filled with his glory!"

ISAIAH 6:1–3 NLT

■ For the LORD, the Most High, is to be feared, a great king over all the earth.

PSALM 47:2 ESV

■ No one is holy like the LORD!
There is no one besides you;
    there is no Rock like our God.

1 SAMUEL 2:2 NLT

■ Then Moses said to Aaron, "This is what the
LORD meant when he said, 'I will display my
holiness through those who come near me.
I will display my glory before all the people.' "
And Aaron was silent.

LEVITICUS 10:3 NLT

■ "See now that I myself am He! There is no
god besides me. I put to death and I bring
to life, I have wounded and I will heal, and no
one can deliver out of my hand."

DEUTERONOMY 32:39 NIV

■ But I, by your great mercy, will come into your
house; in reverence will I bow down toward
your holy temple.

PSALM 5:7 NIV

PRAISING GOD

I will exalt you, my God and King, and praise
your name forever and ever.

I will praise you every day; yes, I will praise
you forever. Great is the LORD! He is
most worthy of praise!

No one can measure his greatness.

Let each generation tell its children of your
mighty acts; let them proclaim your
power.

I will meditate on your majestic, glorious
splendor and your wonderful miracles.

Your awe-inspiring deeds will be on every
tongue; I will proclaim your greatness.

Everyone will share the story of your
wonderful goodness; they will sing with
joy about your righteousness.

The LORD is merciful and compassionate, slow
to get angry and filled with unfailing love.

The LORD is good to everyone. He showers
compassion on all his creation.

PSALM 145:1–9 NLT

53

■ Each of the four living creatures had six wings and was covered with eyes all around, even under his wings. Day and night they never stop saying: "Holy, holy, holy is the Lord God Almighty, who was, and is, and is to come."

REVELATION 4:8 NIV

■ Praise the LORD! Praise God in his sanctuary;
    praise him in his mighty heavens!
Praise him for his mighty deeds;
    praise him according to his excellent
    greatness!
Praise him with trumpet sound;
    praise him with lute and harp!
Praise him with tambourine and dance;
    praise him with strings and pipe!
Praise him with sounding cymbals;
    praise him with loud clashing cymbals!
Let everything that has breath praise the
    LORD! Praise the LORD!

PSALM 150:1–6 ESV

But I will hope continually and will praise you yet more and more.

PSALM 71:14 ESV

Praise the LORD.
Praise, O servants of the LORD,
    praise the name of the LORD.
Let the name of the LORD be praised,
    both now and forevermore.
From the rising of the sun to the place
    where it sets, the name of the LORD
    is to be praised.
The LORD is exalted over all the nations,
    his glory above the heavens.
Who is like the LORD our God,
    the One who sits enthroned on high,
    who stoops down to look on the
    heavens and the earth?

PSALM 113:1–6 NIV

ONE MOMENT
AT A TIME

GETTING YOUR
EYES ON GOD

■ **Get outdoors.** One of the best ways to glimpse the majesty of God is to get outdoors and see His great creation. Spend an hour outside praying in a place where you can enjoy the sky, trees, ocean, or a river. As you pray, remind yourself of the God who made it all and is worthy of your deepest praise.

■ **Make music.** While we enjoy reading the Psalms of praise from the Bible, we tend to forget these words were originally written as lyrics to music. Find a hymn or song of worship you can sing to God, or sing along to a praise tape as a way of prompting your time of praise.

Begin a prayer journal. Many people are easily distracted during prayer. One practical way to beat those distractions is to write out what you want to say to God. Try taking a simple sheet of paper with you and using it to write down your prayer of praise. You may be surprised at how this helps you to remain focused. If the exercise works, consider creating a prayer journal and making this activity a regular part of your prayer time.

CHAPTER 4

THE PRAYER OF CONFESSION

I fail God so often that confessing my sins comes pretty easy. And when I finally think I'm through confessing them, He brings something else to mind. While I could become quite discouraged by this, it really never turns into the pity party it may sound like. In fact, it's quite the opposite. The more I confess, the more I realize He's holy and I'm driven to praise Him yet again. And as I confess, I realize how great His forgiveness and His love for me is. Nothing feels so good as coming clean with God.

■ Cody, age 36, Florida ■

ACKNOWLEDGING YOUR SIN

■ "When anyone is guilty in any of these ways, he must confess in what way he has sinned."

LEVITICUS 5:5 NIV

■ Lord, open my lips, and my mouth will
declare your praise.
You do not delight in sacrifice, or I would
bring it; you do not take pleasure in
burnt offerings.
The sacrifices of God are a broken spirit;
a broken and contrite heart,
O God, you will not despise.

PSALM 51:15–17 NIV

■ Saul said to Samuel, "I have sinned, for I have transgressed the commandment of the LORD and your words, because I feared the people and obeyed their voice. Now therefore, please pardon my sin and return with me that I may worship the LORD."

1 SAMUEL 15:24–25 ESV

We have sinned, even as our fathers did;
we have done wrong and acted wickedly.

PSALM 106:6 NIV

Search me, O God, and know my heart;
test me and know my anxious thoughts.
See if there is any offensive way in me,
and lead me in the way everlasting.

PSALM 139:23–24 NIV

How many wrongs and sins have I committed?
Show me my offense and my sin.

JOB 13:23 NIV

For our offenses are many in your sight,
        and our sins testify against us.
Our offenses are ever with us,
        and we acknowledge our iniquities:
        rebellion and treachery against the LORD,
        turning our backs on our God,
        fomenting oppression and revolt,
        uttering lies our hearts have conceived.

ISAIAH 59:12–13 NIV

61

We know our wickedness, O LORD,
The iniquity of our fathers, for we have
sinned against You.

JEREMIAH 14:20 NASB

If we claim to be without sin, we deceive
ourselves and the truth is not in us.

1 JOHN 1:8 NIV

As for me, I said, "O LORD, be gracious to me;
Heal my soul, for I have sinned against You."

PSALM 41:4 NASB

"Listen to my prayer! Look down and see me
praying night and day for your people Israel.
I confess that we have sinned against you.
Yes, even my own family and I have sinned!
We have sinned terribly by not obeying the
commands, decrees, and regulations that you
gave us through your servant Moses."

NEHEMIAH 1:6–7 NLT

REQUESTING FORGIVENESS

■ Listen from your home in heaven,
      forgive the sins of your servants,
      your people Israel.
Then start over with them; train them
      to live right and well;
Send rain on the land you gave as
      inheritance to your people.

2 CHRONICLES 6:27 MSG

■ "Listen to the supplications of Your servant
and of Your people Israel when they pray
toward this place; hear from Your dwelling
place, from heaven; hear and forgive. . . . then
hear from heaven and forgive the sin of Your
people Israel, and bring them back to the
land which You have given to them and to
their fathers."

2 CHRONICLES 6:21, 25 NASB

■ Then David said to God, "I have sinned
greatly by doing this. Now, I beg you, take
away the guilt of your servant. I have done a
very foolish thing."

1 CHRONICLES 21:8 NIV

■ Return, O Israel, to the LORD your God,
for your sins have brought you down.
Bring your confessions, and return to
the LORD.
    Say to him, "Forgive all our sins and gra-
ciously receive us, so that we may offer you
our praises."

HOSEA 14:1–2 NLT

■ Listen from your home in heaven to their
        prayers desperate and devout;
Do what is best for them.
Forgive your people who have sinned
        against you.

2 CHRONICLES 6:39 MSG

■ I admit I once lived by rumors of you;
   now I have it all firsthand—from my
   own eyes and ears!
I'm sorry—forgive me. I'll never do that again,
   I promise!
I'll never again live on crusts of hearsay,
   crumbs of rumor.

JOB 42:5–6 MSG

■ Forgive us our debts, as we also have forgiven
our debtors.

MATTHEW 6:12 NIV

■ Then I acknowledged my sin to you and did
not cover up my iniquity. I said, "I will confess
my transgressions to the LORD"—and you
forgave the guilt of my sin.

PSALM 32:5 NIV

EMBRACING FORGIVENESS

■ He will not always accuse, nor will he harbor his anger forever; he does not treat us as our sins deserve or repay us according to our iniquities.

For as high as the heavens are above the earth, so great is his love for those who fear him; as far as the east is from the west, so far has he removed our transgressions from us.

As a father has compassion on his children, so the LORD has compassion on those who fear him.

PSALM 103:9–13 NIV

■ My sins will be stuffed in a sack and thrown into the sea—sunk in deep ocean.

JOB 14:17 MSG

If you, O LORD, kept a record of sins,
    O Lord, who could stand?
But with you there is forgiveness;
    therefore you are feared.

PSALM 130:3–4 NIV

Who may ascend into the hill of the LORD?
And who may stand in His holy place?
He who has clean hands and a pure heart,
Who has not lifted up his soul to falsehood,
And has not sworn deceitfully.
He shall receive a blessing from the LORD
And righteousness from the God of his
    salvation.

PSALM 24:3–5 NASB

"Come now, let's settle this," says the LORD.
"Though your sins are like scarlet,
I will make them as white as snow.
Though they are red like crimson,
I will make them as white as wool."

ISAIAH 1:18 NLT

■ I have swept away your offenses like a cloud,
your sins like the morning mist. Return to me,
for I have redeemed you.

ISAIAH 44:22 NIV

■ "No longer will a man teach his neighbor, or
a man his brother, saying, 'Know the LORD,'
because they will all know me, from the least
of them to the greatest," declares the LORD.
"For I will forgive their wickedness and will
remember their sins no more."

JEREMIAH 31:34 NIV

CONFESSING SIN

Remember not the sins of my youth or
    my transgressions; according to your
steadfast love remember me, for the sake
    of your goodness, O LORD!
Good and upright is the LORD;
    therefore he instructs sinners in the way.
He leads the humble in what is right,
    and teaches the humble his way.
All the paths of the LORD are steadfast
    love and faithfulness, for those who
    keep his covenant and his testimonies.
For your name's sake, O LORD,
    pardon my guilt, for it is great.
Who is the man who fears the LORD?
Him will he instruct in the way that he
    should choose.
His soul shall abide in well-being,
    and his offspring shall inherit the land.
The friendship of the LORD is for those who
    fear him, and he makes known to them
    his covenant.

My eyes are ever toward the LORD,
    for he will pluck my feet out of the net.
Turn to me and be gracious to me,
    for I am lonely and afflicted.
The troubles of my heart are enlarged;
    bring me out of my distresses.
Consider my affliction and my trouble,
    and forgive all my sins.

PSALM 25:7–18 ESV

Wash away all my iniquity and cleanse me
from my sin. For I know my transgressions,
and my sin is always before me. Against you,
you only, have I sinned and done what is evil
in your sight, so that you are proved right
when you speak and justified when you
judge. Surely I was sinful at birth, sinful from
the time my mother conceived me. Surely
you desire truth in the inner parts; you teach
me wisdom in the inmost place. Cleanse me
with hyssop, and I will be clean; wash me, and
I will be whiter than snow.

PSALM 51:2–7 NIV

For I know that nothing good dwells in me, that is, in my flesh. For I have the desire to do what is right, but not the ability to carry it out. For I do not do the good I want, but the evil I do not want is what I keep on doing. Now if I do what I do not want, it is no longer I who do it, but sin that dwells within me.

So I find it to be a law that when I want to do right, evil lies close at hand. For I delight in the law of God, in my inner being, but I see in my members another law waging war against the law of my mind and making me captive to the law of sin that dwells in my members. Wretched man that I am! Who will deliver me from this body of death? Thanks be to God through Jesus Christ our Lord!

ROMANS 7:18–25 ESV

If we confess our sins, he is faithful and just and will forgive us our sins and purify us from all unrighteousness.

1 JOHN 1:9 NIV

ONE MOMENT
AT A TIME
COMING CLEAN

Destroy the list. Give yourself a visual picture of what God's forgiveness means. As you pray, write down a list of sins you need to confess. When you've finished, take the list and destroy it—perhaps shred it or safely burn it. Let that image illustrate the way God has removed your sins from His record.

Review the day. While guilt and confession come easily for some people, others move so quickly through their day that they can't come up with much to confess. Review the last twenty-four hours and remember the places you went, conversations you had, and attitudes you felt. If Jesus were physically standing next to you, what interactions or thoughts would make you blush? Those may be good indications of areas needing confession.

Find accountability. If you find yourself quick to gossip, grow angry, or succumb to another sin regularly, ask a close friend to help keep you accountable to changing in this area. With a little help from a friend, maybe you will be able to confess this sin a little less often.

CHAPTER 5

THE PRAYER OF THANKSGIVING

A few weeks ago I was in church and heard the pastor speak about being thankful. As I listened, it struck me that I hadn't said "thank you" to God in a really, really long time. I'm fairly quick to ask for His help, but I'm not so fast when it comes to being grateful. Since then, I've been very purposeful about being thankful. I've been thanking God for the big things as well as the little things. When I got my latest sales bonus, I thanked God. When my car started this morning, I thanked God. I've realized that every blessing comes from God and I've been doing much better at acknowledging that.

■ Pamela, age 48, Missouri ■

BEING INTENTIONAL IN THANKS

■ This is the day the LORD has made;
let us rejoice and be glad in it.

PSALM 118:24 NIV

■ Devote yourselves to prayer with an alert
mind and a thankful heart.

COLOSSIANS 4:2 NLT

■ Then David assigned some of the Levites
to the Chest of GOD to lead worship—to
intercede, give thanks, and praise the GOD of
Israel.

1 CHRONICLES 16:4 MSG

■ O give thanks to the LORD, for He is good;
For His lovingkindness is everlasting.

1 CHRONICLES 16:34 NASB

I will give you thanks in the great assembly;
among throngs of people I will praise you.

PSALM 35:18 NIV

Now, our God, we give you thanks,
and praise your glorious name.

1 CHRONICLES 29:13 NIV

After consulting the people, Jehoshaphat
appointed men to sing to the LORD and to
praise him for the splendor of his holiness as
they went out at the head of the army, saying:
"Give thanks to the LORD, for his love
endures forever."

2 CHRONICLES 20:21 NIV

Give thanks to the LORD, for he is good; ...
Let them give thanks to the LORD for his unfailing love and his wonderful deeds for men.

PSALM 107:1, 8 NIV

Rejoice always.

1 THESSALONIANS 5:16 NASB

THANKING GOD FOR SALVATION

■ Open to me the gates of righteousness;
I shall enter through them, I shall give thanks
to the LORD.

PSALM 118:19 NASB

■ I delight greatly in the LORD; my soul rejoices
in my God.

For he has clothed me with garments of
salvation and arrayed me in a robe of righteousness, as a bridegroom adorns his head
like a priest, and as a bride adorns herself
with her jewels.

ISAIAH 61:10 NIV

■ Save us, O God of our salvation,
and gather and deliver us from among the
nations, that we may give thanks to your holy
name, and glory in your praise.

1 CHRONICLES 16:35 ESV

I am grateful that God always makes it possible for Christ to lead us to victory. God also helps us spread the knowledge about Christ everywhere, and this knowledge is like the smell of perfume.

2 CORINTHIANS 2:14 CEV

I pray that you will be grateful to God for letting you have part in what he has promised his people in the kingdom of light.

COLOSSIANS 1:12 CEV

All the angels were standing around the throne and around the elders and the four living creatures. They fell down on their faces before the throne and worshiped God, saying: "Amen!

Praise and glory and wisdom and thanks and honor and power and strength be to our God for ever and ever. Amen!"

REVELATION 7:11–12 NIV

APPRECIATING HIS KINDNESS

■ We give thanks to you, O God,
we give thanks, for your Name is near;
men tell of your wonderful deeds.

PSALM 75:1 NIV

■ So thank GOD for his marvelous love,
for his miracle mercy to the children
he loves.

PSALM 107:31 MSG

■ I will tell of the kindnesses of the LORD, the deeds for which he is to be praised, according to all the LORD has done for us—yes, the many good things he has done for the house of Israel, according to his compassion and many kindnesses.

ISAIAH 63:7 NIV

Sing to the LORD!
    Praise the LORD!
For though I was poor and needy,
    he rescued me from my oppressors.

JEREMIAH 20:13 NLT

Shout for joy, O heavens; rejoice, O earth;
burst into song, O mountains! For the LORD
comforts his people and will have compassion on his afflicted ones.

ISAIAH 49:13 NIV

I will praise you, LORD!
    You always do right.
I will sing about you,
    the LORD Most High.

PSALM 7:17 CEV

81

BEING GRATEFUL IN EVERYTHING

▓ And whatever you do, whether in word or deed, do it all in the name of the Lord Jesus, giving thanks to God the Father through him.

COLOSSIANS 3:17 NIV

▓ Give thanks in all circumstances; for this is the will of God in Christ Jesus for you.

1 THESSALONIANS 5:18 ESV

▓ I will sing to the LORD, for he has been good to me.

PSALM 13:6 NIV

▓ More joy in one ordinary day than they get in all their shopping sprees.
At day's end I'm ready for sound sleep,
for you, God, have put my life back together.

PSALM 4:7–8 MSG

Speak to one another with psalms, hymns and spiritual songs. Sing and make music in your heart to the Lord, always giving thanks to God the Father for everything, in the name of our Lord Jesus Christ.

EPHESIANS 5:19–20 NIV

ENJOYING ANSWERED PRAYERS

■ And you will say in that day: "Give thanks to the LORD, call upon his name, make known his deeds among the peoples, proclaim that his name is exalted.

Sing praises to the LORD, for he has done gloriously; let this be made known in all the earth."

ISAIAH 12:4–5 ESV

■ "I thank and praise you, O God of my fathers: You have given me wisdom and power, you have made known to me what we asked of you, you have made known to us the dream of the king."

DANIEL 2:23 NIV

■ "Praise be to the LORD, who has given rest to his people Israel just as he promised. Not one word has failed of all the good promises he gave through his servant Moses."

1 KINGS 8:56 NIV

■ We cried out to the LORD, the God of our
fathers, and the LORD heard our voice and
saw our misery, toil and oppression. So the
LORD brought us out of Egypt with a mighty
hand and an outstretched arm, with great
terror and with miraculous signs and
wonders.

DEUTERONOMY 26:7–8 NIV

■ I will praise you, LORD, with all my heart;
I will tell of all the marvelous things you have
    done.
I will be filled with joy because of you.
I will sing praises to your name, O Most High.

PSALM 9:1–2 NLT

■ I love you, O LORD, my strength. The LORD is
    my rock, my fortress and my deliverer;
    my God is my rock, in whom I take refuge.
He is my shield and the horn of my
    salvation, my stronghold.

PSALM 18:1–2 NIV

VALUING THE PEOPLE IN YOUR LIFE

■ We always thank God, the Father of our Lord Jesus Christ, when we pray for you, because we have heard of your faith in Christ Jesus and of the love you have for all the saints.

COLOSSIANS 1:3–4 NIV

■ Every time I think of you, I give thanks to my God. Whenever I pray, I make my requests for all of you with joy, for you have been my partners in spreading the Good News about Christ from the time you first heard it until now.

PHILIPPIANS 1:3–5 NLT

■ I always thank my God as I remember you in my prayers.

PHILEMON 1:4 NIV

■ I thank my God always concerning you for the grace of God which was given to you by Christ Jesus.

1 CORINTHIANS 1:4 NKJV

■ Ever since I first heard of your strong faith in the Lord Jesus and your love for God's people everywhere, I have not stopped thanking God for you. I pray for you constantly.

EPHESIANS 1:15–16 NLT

■ We always thank God for all of you, mentioning you in our prayers.

1 THESSALONIANS 1:2 NIV

ONE MOMENT
AT A TIME
COUNT YOUR
BLESSINGS

Learn to be thankful. Put a 3" x 5" card in
your wallet or in your pocket. As good things
happen to you throughout the day, take a
moment and write them down. At your next
time of prayer, pull out the list and thank God
for all He's done for you in the last day.

Keep a running tally. Consider creating a
prayer journal that records both prayer
requests and answers to prayer. Be sure
to take time to thank God for every prayer
He answers.

Give T-H-A-N-K-S. Use an acronym like the word *thanks* to organize and prompt your prayer. Think of an area of your life (such as your job or your family) and thank God for different things that begin with each letter of the word you've chosen.

CHAPTER 6

THE PRAYER OF SUPPLICATION

I used to think that asking God to meet my needs was selfish. My logic was that I should spend time praising God for who He is and thanking Him for the blessings in my life. The more I read the Bible, however, the more I realized that the Bible is filled with instructions to ask God for help. Finally it hit me that not asking God for help was pretty prideful of me. I can't control my health, my family, or my job status. What I can control is my faithfulness to God and my effort to humbly bring my requests before the One who holds today's outcomes in His hands.

■ Kenneth, age 51, Arizona ■

REQUESTING HEALING

■ Heal me, O LORD, and I will be healed;
Save me and I will be saved,
For You are my praise.

JEREMIAH 17:14 NASB

■ LORD my God,
I cried to You for help, and You healed me.

PSALM 30:2 NASB

■ Dear friend, I pray that you may enjoy good
health and that all may go well with you, even
as your soul is getting along well.

3 JOHN 2 NIV

■ Have compassion on me, LORD, for I am weak.
Heal me, LORD, for my bones are in agony.

PSALM 6:2 NLT

Bless the LORD, O my soul,
    and forget not all his benefits,
who forgives all your iniquity,
who heals all your diseases,
who redeems your life from the pit,
who crowns you with steadfast love
    and mercy,
who satisfies you with good
    so that your youth is renewed like
    the eagle's.

PSALM 103:2–5 ESV

ASKING FOR PROTECTION

■ "Hear, O Lord, the cry of Judah;
   bring him to his people.
   With his own hands he defends his cause.
   Oh, be his help against his foes!"

Deuteronomy 33:7 niv

■ Asa called to the Lord his God and said,
   "Lord, there is no one like you to help the
   powerless against the mighty. Help us, O
   Lord our God, for we rely on you, and in
   your name we have come against this vast
   army. O Lord, you are our God; do not let
   man prevail against you."

2 Chronicles 14:11 niv

■ I call upon the Lord, who is worthy to be
   praised, and I am saved from my enemies.

Psalm 18:3 esv

■ Don't let those proud and merciless people
kick me around or chase me away.

PSALM 36:11 CEV

■ In times of trouble, may the LORD answer
your cry. May the name of the God of Jacob
keep you safe from all harm.

PSALM 20:1 NLT

■ LORD my God, in you do I take refuge;
save me from all my pursuers and deliver me.

PSALM 7:1 ESV

■ Deliver me from my enemies, O God;
protect me from those who rise up
against me.
Deliver me from evildoers and save me from
bloodthirsty men.

PSALM 59:1–2 NIV

■ Deliver me, O LORD, from evil men;
　　preserve me from violent men,
　　who plan evil things in their heart
　　and stir up wars continually.
They make their tongue sharp as a serpent's,
　　and under their lips is the venom of asps.
Selah
Guard me, O LORD, from the hands of the
　　wicked; preserve me from violent men,
　　who have planned to trip up my feet.

PSALM 140:1–4 ESV

■ Please rescue me from my enemies, LORD!
I come to you for safety.

PSALM 143:9 CEV

■ My times are in your hands; deliver me from
my enemies and from those who pursue me.

PSALM 31:15 NIV

SEEKING DELIVERANCE DURING ADVERSITY

Vindicate me, O God, and plead my cause against an ungodly nation; rescue me from deceitful and wicked men.

You are God my stronghold. Why have you rejected me?

Why must I go about mourning, oppressed by the enemy?

Send forth your light and your truth, let them guide me; let them bring me to your holy mountain, to the place where you dwell.

PSALM 43:1–3 NIV

Vindicate me in your righteousness, O LORD my God; do not let them gloat over me.

PSALM 35:24 NIV

■ In you, O LORD, I have taken refuge; let me
        never be put to shame.
Rescue me and deliver me in your
        righteousness; turn your ear to me
        and save me.
Be my rock of refuge, to which I can always
        go; give the command to save me,
        for you are my rock and my fortress.
Deliver me, O my God, from the hand of the
        wicked, from the grasp of evil and cruel
        men.

PSALM 71:1–4 NIV

■ Come with great power, O God,
        and rescue me!
Defend me with your might.
Listen to my prayer, O God.
Pay attention to my plea.
For strangers are attacking me;
        violent people are trying to kill me.
They care nothing for God.
But God is my helper.
The Lord keeps me alive!

PSALM 54:1–4 NLT

FINDING HELP

This poor man called, and the LORD heard
    him; he saved him out of all his troubles.
The angel of the LORD encamps around those
    who fear him, and he delivers them.

PSALM 34:6–7 NIV

Israel, no other god is like ours—
    the clouds are his chariot as he rides
    across the skies to come and help us.
The eternal God is our hiding place;
    he carries us in his arms.
When God tells you to destroy your
    enemies, he will make them run.

DEUTERONOMY 33:26–27 CEV

You are my hiding place; you will protect me
from trouble and surround me with songs of
deliverance.

PSALM 32:7 NIV

We wait in hope for the LORD; he is our help and our shield.

PSALM 33:20 NIV

You, LORD, never fail to have pity on me; your love and faithfulness always keep me secure.

PSALM 40:11 CEV

But you, O LORD, be not far off; O my Strength, come quickly to help me.

PSALM 22:19 NIV

In my distress I called upon the LORD, And cried to my God for help; He heard my voice out of His temple, And my cry for help before Him came into His ears.

PSALM 18:6 NASB

PRAYING DURING TROUBLED TIMES

Hear my prayer, O LORD;
    let my cry come to you!
Do not hide your face from me
    in the day of my distress!
Incline your ear to me;
    answer me speedily in the day
    when I call!

PSALM 102:1–2 ESV

Cast your cares on the LORD and he will sustain you; he will never let the righteous fall.

PSALM 55:22 NIV

Be not far from me, for trouble is near;
For there is none to help.

PSALM 22:11 NASB

■ As for God, his way is perfect; the word of the LORD is flawless. He is a shield for all who take refuge in him.

PSALM 18:30 NIV

■ In my distress I called to the LORD, and he answered me.

PSALM 120:1 ESV

■ In my anguish I cried to the LORD, and he answered by setting me free.

PSALM 118:5 NIV

■ You were in serious trouble, but you prayed to the LORD, and he rescued you.

PSALM 107:6 CEV

■ Call upon me in the day of trouble; I will deliver you, and you will honor me.

PSALM 50:15 NIV

■ Make haste, O God, to deliver me! O LORD, make haste to help me!

PSALM 70:1 ESV

Answer me when I call to you, O my righteous God. Give me relief from my distress; be merciful to me and hear my prayer.

PSALM 4:1 NIV

The troubles of my heart have multiplied; free me from my anguish.

PSALM 25:17 NIV

I cry aloud to God, aloud to God, and he will hear me.

In the day of my trouble I seek the Lord; in the night my hand is stretched out without wearying; my soul refuses to be comforted.

When I remember God, I moan; when I meditate, my spirit faints.
Selah

You hold my eyelids open; I am so troubled that I cannot speak.

PSALM 77:1–4 ESV

103

■ Don't hide from your servant;
answer me quickly, for I am in deep trouble!

PSALM 69:17 NLT

■ The righteous cry out, and the LORD hears
them; he delivers them from all their troubles.

PSALM 34:17 NIV

■ The thought of my suffering and
homelessness is bitter beyond words.
I will never forget this awful time, as I grieve
over my loss.
Yet I still dare to hope when I remember this:
The faithful love of the LORD never ends!
His mercies never cease.
Great is his faithfulness; his mercies begin
afresh each morning.
I say to myself, "The LORD is my inheritance;
therefore, I will hope in him!"

LAMENTATIONS 3:19–24 NLT

■ Because of the extravagance of those revelations, and so I wouldn't get a big head, I was given the gift of a handicap to keep me in constant touch with my limitations. Satan's angel did his best to get me down; what he in fact did was push me to my knees. No danger then of walking around high and mighty! At first I didn't think of it as a gift, and begged God to remove it. Three times I did that, and then he told me, My grace is enough; it's all you need. My strength comes into its own in your weakness.

Once I heard that, I was glad to let it happen. I quit focusing on the handicap and began appreciating the gift. It was a case of Christ's strength moving in on my weakness. Now I take limitations in stride, and with good cheer, these limitations that cut me down to size—abuse, accidents, opposition, bad breaks. I just let Christ take over! And so the weaker I get, the stronger I become.

2 CORINTHIANS 12:7–10 MSG

■ I wait for your salvation, O LORD,
and I follow your commands.

PSALM 119:166 NIV

■ Wait for the LORD;
be strong and take heart
and wait for the LORD.

PSALM 27:14 NIV

REQUESTING PROVISION

For he delivers the needy when he calls,
the poor and him who has no helper.

PSALM 72:12 ESV

Which one of you fathers would give your
hungry child a snake if the child asked for
a fish?

LUKE 11:11 CEV

"This, then, is how you should pray:
Our Father in heaven,
     hallowed be your name, . . .
Give us today our daily bread."

MATTHEW 6:9, 11 NIV

Then, turning to his disciples, Jesus said, "That
is why I tell you not to worry about everyday
life—whether you have enough food to eat
or enough clothes to wear. For life is more
than food, and your body more than clothing. Look at the ravens. They don't plant or

harvest or store food in barns, for God feeds them. And you are far more valuable to him than any birds! Can all your worries add a single moment to your life? And if worry can't accomplish a little thing like that, what's the use of worrying over bigger things?

"Look at the lilies and how they grow. They don't work or make their clothing, yet Solomon in all his glory was not dressed as beautifully as they are. And if God cares so wonderfully for flowers that are here today and thrown into the fire tomorrow, he will certainly care for you. Why do you have so little faith?

"And don't be concerned about what to eat and what to drink. Don't worry about such things. These things dominate the thoughts of unbelievers all over the world, but your Father already knows your needs. Seek the Kingdom of God above all else, and he will give you everything you need."

LUKE 12:22–31 NLT

SEEKING SUCCESS

Please, LORD, please save us.
Please, LORD, please give us success.

PSALM 118:25 NLT

Jabez cried out to the God of Israel, "Oh, that you would bless me and enlarge my territory! Let your hand be with me, and keep me from harm so that I will be free from pain." And God granted his request.

1 CHRONICLES 4:10 NIV

"O Lord, let your ear be attentive to the prayer of this your servant and to the prayer of your servants who delight in revering your name. Give your servant success today by granting him favor in the presence of this man."

NEHEMIAH 1:11 NIV

REMEMBERING THE ELDERLY

■ Do not cast me off in the time of old age;
forsake me not when my strength is spent.

PSALM 71:9 ESV

■ Be merciful to me, O LORD, for I am in
distress; my eyes grow weak with sorrow,
my soul and my body with grief.
  My life is consumed by anguish and
my years by groaning; my strength fails because of my affliction, and my bones
grow weak.

PSALM 31:9–10 NIV

■ For you, O Lord, are my hope,
my trust, O LORD, from my youth.

PSALM 71:5 ESV

And I'll keep on carrying you when
you're old.
I'll be there, bearing you when you're
old and gray.
I've done it and will keep on doing it,
carrying you on my back, saving you.

ISAIAH 46:4 MSG

ONE MOMENT
AT A TIME

BRINGING YOUR
REQUESTS
TO GOD

Make one-sentence prayers a habit. Prayer time doesn't always need to be long. Get comfortable offering God short, one-sentence prayers during the day when you need His help. No matter the setting, take a moment to pray when you face your next challenge.

Turn off the electronics. Radios, cell phones, and MP3 players offer constant distraction. During an upcoming drive in your car, turn everything off and pray in silence while you make your trip. Or if you're at home, leave the cell phone off and in the other room as you spend time bringing your requests to your heavenly Father.

Set a timer. Try to find a block of time where you can pray without encountering great distraction. Pray without keeping an eye on the clock and without worrying about what you might need to do next. If you have some place to be, then set a timer nearby to indicate when your time needs to be done. Until it goes off, spend undistracted one-on-one time with God.

CHAPTER 7

PRAYERS OF THE HEART

I take a lot of comfort in Romans 8, which reads, "We do not know what we ought to pray for, but the Spirit himself intercedes for us with groans that words cannot express." Sometimes I'm so confused or broken up over a situation that I don't know how to pray. I'm not sure how to deal with the pain or what the right answer is to the problem I'm facing. During those difficult moments, I sometimes just spend time crying in God's presence. And while I can leave those prayers without feeling like I actually prayed many specific words, it's enough for me to know that God sees my heart and hears my groans.

■ Jackie, age 41, California ■

AVOIDING TEMPTATION

■ "Keep watching and praying that you may not enter into temptation; the spirit is willing, but the flesh is weak."

MATTHEW 26:41 NASB

■ There he told them, "Pray that you will not give in to temptation."

LUKE 22:40 NLT

■ Create in me a clean heart, O God,
And renew a steadfast spirit within me.

PSALM 51:10 NASB

■ Submit yourselves, then, to God. Resist the devil, and he will flee from you.

JAMES 4:7 NIV

■ LORD, be gracious to us; we long for you.
Be our strength every morning, our salvation in time of distress.

ISAIAH 33:2 NIV

EXPERIENCING JOY

■ The LORD is my strength and my shield;
my heart trusts in him, and I am helped.
My heart leaps for joy and I will give thanks
to him in song.

PSALM 28:7 NIV

■ Sing the glory of his name; give to him
glorious praise!
Say to God, "How awesome are your deeds!
So great is your power that your enemies
come cringing to you."

PSALM 66:2–3 ESV

■ Let the righteous rejoice in the LORD
and take refuge in him; let all the upright in
heart praise him!

PSALM 64:10 NIV

■ "Until now you have asked nothing in my
name. Ask, and you will receive, that your joy
may be full."

JOHN 16:24 ESV

■ Why are you cast down, O my soul?
And why are you disquieted within me?
Hope in God; For I shall yet praise Him,
The help of my countenance and my God.

PSALM 42:11 NKJV

■ Though the fig tree should not blossom, nor
fruit be on the vines, the produce of the olive
fail and the fields yield no food, the flock be
cut off from the fold and there be no herd
in the stalls, yet I will rejoice in the LORD;
I will take joy in the God of my salvation.
GOD, the Lord, is my strength; he makes my
feet like the deer's; he makes me tread on my
high places.

HABAKKUK 3:17–19 ESV

HOPING FOR GRACE AND MERCY

▪ Therefore let us draw near with confidence to the throne of grace, so that we may receive mercy and find grace to help in time of need.

HEBREWS 4:16 NASB

▪ Hear my prayer, O LORD;
listen to my cry for mercy.

PSALM 86:6 NIV

▪ I love God because he listened to me,
listened as I begged for mercy.

PSALM 116:1 MSG

▪ And God is able to make all grace abound to you, so that in all things at all times, having all that you need, you will abound in every good work.

2 CORINTHIANS 9:8 NIV

Hear my prayer, O Lord; give ear to my pleas for mercy!
In your faithfulness answer me, in your righteousness!

PSALM 143:1 ESV

But grow in the grace and knowledge of our Lord and Savior Jesus Christ. To him be glory both now and forever! Amen.

2 PETER 3:18 NIV

I say to the Lord, You are my God;
give ear to the voice of my pleas for mercy,
O Lord!

PSALM 140:6 ESV

Grace, mercy and peace from God the Father and from Jesus Christ, the Father's Son, will be with us in truth and love.

2 JOHN 3 NIV

SEARCHING FOR PEACE

I pray that God will be kind to you and will let you live in perfect peace! May you keep learning more and more about God and our Lord Jesus.

2 PETER 1:2 CEV

"The LORD bless you and keep you; the LORD make his face to shine upon you and be gracious to you; the LORD lift up his countenance upon you and give you peace."

NUMBERS 6:24–26 ESV

Come to Me, all who are weary and heavy-laden, and I will give you rest.

MATTHEW 11:28 NASB

Be my rock of safety where I can always hide. Give the order to save me, for you are my rock and my fortress.

PSALM 71:3 NLT

121

■ In peace I will lie down and sleep,
   for you alone, O LORD, will keep me safe.

PSALM 4:8 NLT

■ But now, O Jacob, listen to the LORD
      who created you.
   O Israel, the one who formed you says,
      "Do not be afraid, for I have
      ransomed you.
   I have called you by name; you are mine.
   When you go through deep waters,
      I will be with you.
   When you go through rivers of difficulty,
      you will not drown.
   When you walk through the fire of
      oppression, you will not be burned up;
      the flames will not consume you.
   For I am the LORD, your God,
      the Holy One of Israel, your Savior.
   I gave Egypt as a ransom for your freedom;
      I gave Ethiopia and Seba in your place."

ISAIAH 43:1–3 NLT

Do not be anxious about anything, but in everything, by prayer and petition, with thanksgiving, present your requests to God. And the peace of God, which transcends all understanding, will guard your hearts and your minds in Christ Jesus.

PHILIPPIANS 4:6–7 NIV

LONGING FOR SPIRITUAL GROWTH

■ Praise be to you, O Lord; teach me your decrees.

PSALM 119:12 NIV

■ May the words of my mouth and the meditation of my heart be pleasing to you, O Lord, my rock and my redeemer.

PSALM 19:14 NLT

■ And we pray...that you may live a life worthy of the Lord and may please him in every way: bearing fruit in every good work, growing in the knowledge of God, being strengthened with all power according to his glorious might so that you may have great endurance and patience.

COLOSSIANS 1:10–11 NIV

Teach me to do Your will,
    For You are my God;
Your Spirit is good.
    Lead me in the land of uprightness.

PSALM 143:10 NKJV

I recounted my ways and you answered me;
    teach me your decrees.
Let me understand the teaching of
    your precepts; then I will meditate
    on your wonders.

PSALM 119:26–27 NIV

Teach me your decrees, O LORD;
    I will keep them to the end.
Give me understanding and I will obey
    your instructions;
I will put them into practice with all
    my heart.

PSALM 119:33–34 NLT

■ I believe in your commands; now teach me
    good judgment and knowledge.
I used to wander off until you disciplined me;
    but now I closely follow your word.
You are good and do only good;
    teach me your decrees.

PSALM 119:66–68 NLT

■ Like newborn babies, you must crave pure
spiritual milk so that you will grow into a
full experience of salvation. Cry out for this
nourishment, now that you have had a taste
of the Lord's kindness.

1 PETER 2:2–3 NLT

■ Teach me how to live, O LORD.
Lead me along the right path,
    for my enemies are waiting for me.

PSALM 27:11 NLT

■ Show me your ways, O LORD,
    teach me your paths.

PSALM 25:4 NIV

God, listen to me shout,
  bend an ear to my prayer.
When I'm far from anywhere,
  down to my last gasp,
I call out, "Guide me
  up High Rock Mountain!"

PSALM 61:1–2 MSG

Guard my life and rescue me;
  let me not be put to shame,
  for I take refuge in you.
May integrity and uprightness protect me,
  because my hope is in you.

PSALM 25:20–21 NIV

127

NEEDING COMFORT

My soul is weary with sorrow;
strengthen me according to your word.

PSALM 119:28 NIV

Even though I walk through the valley
of the shadow of death, I will fear no evil,
for you are with me; your rod and
your staff, they comfort me.

PSALM 23:4 NIV

All praise to God, the Father of our Lord
Jesus Christ. God is our merciful Father and
the source of all comfort. He comforts us
in all our troubles so that we can comfort
others. When they are troubled, we will be
able to give them the same comfort God
has given us.

2 CORINTHIANS 1:3–4 NLT

I will comfort you there in Jerusalem
as a mother comforts her child.

ISAIAH 66:13 NLT

As the deer pants for the water brooks,
    So my soul pants for You, O God.
My soul thirsts for God, for the living God;
    When shall I come and appear before
    God?

PSALM 42:1–2 NASB

My groaning has worn me out.
At night my bed and pillow are soaked
    with tears.
Sorrow has made my eyes dim,
    and my sight has failed because of
    my enemies.
You, LORD, heard my crying.

PSALM 6:6–8 CEV

FEELING LONELY

■ Turn to me and be gracious to me,
for I am lonely and afflicted.

PSALM 25:16 NIV

■ "Do not fear, for I am with you;
Do not anxiously look about you,
for I am your God.
I will strengthen you, surely I will help you,
Surely I will uphold you with
My righteous right hand."

ISAIAH 41:10 NASB

■ Our LORD, you bless those who join in
the festival and walk in the brightness
of your presence.

PSALM 89:15 CEV

■ For I hold you by your right hand—
      I, the LORD your God.
And I say to you,
      "Don't be afraid. I am here to help you."

ISAIAH 41:13 NLT

■ The LORD is with me; I will not be afraid.
What can man do to me?
The LORD is with me; he is my helper.
I will look in triumph on my enemies.
It is better to take refuge in the LORD
      than to trust in man.

PSALM 118:6–8 NIV

■ Where can I go from your Spirit?
Where can I flee from your presence?

PSALM 139:7 NIV

FINDING HOPE

May your unfailing love rest upon us, O LORD,
even as we put our hope in you.

PSALM 33:22 NIV

"And now, Lord, for what do I wait?
My hope is in You."

PSALM 39:7 NASB

No one whose hope is in you will ever be
put to shame, but they will be put to shame
who are treacherous without excuse.

PSALM 25:3 NIV

Hear my cry for mercy as I call to you for
help, as I lift up my hands toward your
Most Holy Place.

PSALM 28:2 NIV

Why am I discouraged?
Why is my heart so sad?
I will put my hope in God!
I will praise him again—
my Savior and my God!

PSALM 42:5–6 NLT

I waited patiently for the LORD;
 he turned to me and heard my cry.
He lifted me out of the slimy pit,
 out of the mud and mire;
 he set my feet on a rock
 and gave me a firm place to stand.
He put a new song in my mouth,
 a hymn of praise to our God.
Many will see and fear and put their trust
 in the LORD.

PSALM 40:1–3 NIV

You are my refuge and my shield;
 I have put my hope in your word.

PSALM 119:114 NIV

From early on your Sanctuary was set high,
    a throne of glory, exalted!
O God, you're the hope of Israel.
All who leave you end up as fools.

JEREMIAH 17:12–13 MSG

It is good to wait quietly for the salvation of
the LORD.

LAMENTATIONS 3:26 NIV

May the God of hope fill you with all joy and
peace in believing, so that by the power of
the Holy Spirit you may abound in hope.

ROMANS 15:13 ESV

Let all that I am wait quietly before God,
for my hope is in him.

PSALM 62:5 NLT

OBTAINING WISDOM

■ If any of you lacks wisdom, he should ask
God, who gives generously to all without
finding fault, and it will be given to him.

JAMES 1:5 NIV

■ Surely you desire truth in the inner parts;
you teach me wisdom in the inmost place.

PSALM 51:6 NIV

■ "Praise be to the name of God for ever
        and ever; wisdom and power are his.
He changes times and seasons;
        he sets up kings and deposes them.
He gives wisdom to the wise
        and knowledge to the discerning."

DANIEL 2:20–21 NIV

That night God appeared to Solomon and said, "What do you want? Ask, and I will give it to you!"

Solomon replied to God, "You showed faithful love to David, my father, and now you have made me king in his place. O LORD God, please continue to keep your promise to David my father, for you have made me king over a people as numerous as the dust of the earth! Give me the wisdom and knowledge to lead them properly, for who could possibly govern this great people of yours?"

God said to Solomon, "Because your greatest desire is to help your people, and you did not ask for wealth, riches, fame, or even the death of your enemies or a long life, but rather you asked for wisdom and knowledge to properly govern my people—I will certainly give you the wisdom and knowledge you requested. But I will also give you wealth, riches, and fame such as no other king has had before you or will ever have in the future!"

2 CHRONICLES 1:7–12 NLT

■ "Call to me and I will answer you and tell you great and unsearchable things you do not know."

JEREMIAH 33:3 NIV

■ Guide me in your truth and teach me, for you are God my Savior, and my hope is in you all day long.

PSALM 25:5 NIV

LOOKING FOR GUIDANCE

For this God is our God for ever and ever;
he will be our guide even to the end.

PSALM 48:14 NIV

Trust in the LORD with all your heart
and lean not on your own understanding;
in all your ways acknowledge him,
and he will make your paths straight.

PROVERBS 3:5–6 NIV

Since you are my rock and my fortress,
for the sake of your name lead and guide me.

PSALM 31:3 NIV

Lead me in the right path, O LORD,
or my enemies will conquer me.
Make your way plain for me to follow.

PSALM 5:8 NLT

■ If I rise on the wings of the dawn,
if I settle on the far side of the sea,
even there your hand will guide me,
your right hand will hold me fast.

PSALM 139:9–10 NIV

■ May the peoples praise you, O God; may all
the peoples praise you. May the nations be
glad and sing for joy, for you rule the peoples
justly and guide the nations of the earth.

PSALM 67:3–4 NIV

■ Direct my footsteps according to your word;
let no sin rule over me.

PSALM 119:133 NIV

ONE MOMENT
AT A TIME

HAVING A
TENDER HEART

- **Pray scripture.** Praying scripture is an ex-
  tremely helpful way to prime your own
  prayers, and it gives you words to pray when
  you don't know what to say. Pull out some
  of the scriptures from this chapter and pray
  them back to God.

- **Pray the Lord's Prayer.** The prayer Jesus
  taught His disciples is found in Matthew
  6:9–13. Use it as a model for your own
  prayer today. As you pray each line, con-
  centrate on its meaning and augment each
  phrase with your own prayer.

Light a candle. While many church tradi-
tions use candles as symbols in their prayers,
others never use them. If you have a specific
need you're praying for, pray as you light the
candle. As the flame goes upward, remember
that your prayer is also heard by God. While
there's nothing magical about a candle, it can
be a useful tool in helping you focus.

CHAPTER 8

PRAYERS FOR OTHERS

I never knew how much my dad prayed for me until I went home between semesters of college. As I moved my bags back into my old room, I noticed some footprints on my floor. When I say footprints, it was really a well-worn path in the carpet between the door of my room and the head of my bed. I pointed to them and asked my mom what caused the spots on the carpet. She told me that my dad would come into my room at least twice a day to pray for me while I was away.

■ Kelly, age 20, Kentucky ■

HEEDING THE CALL

■ "As for me, far be it from me that I should sin against the LORD by failing to pray for you. And I will teach you the way that is good and right."

1 SAMUEL 12:23 NIV

■ If you see a Christian brother or sister sinning in a way that does not lead to death, you should pray, and God will give that person life. But there is a sin that leads to death, and I am not saying you should pray for those who commit it.

1 JOHN 5:16 NLT

■ Pray for us, for our conscience is clear and we want to live honorably in everything we do.

HEBREWS 13:18 NLT

I thank God, whom I serve, as my forefathers did, with a clear conscience, as night and day I constantly remember you in my prayers.

2 TIMOTHY 1:3 NIV

LIFTING UP YOUR CHILDREN

May the LORD make you increase,
　　both you and your children.
May you be blessed by the LORD,
　　the Maker of heaven and earth.

PSALM 115:14–15 NIV

When a period of feasting had run its
course, Job would send and have them
purified. Early in the morning he would
sacrifice a burnt offering for each of them,
thinking, "Perhaps my children have sinned
and cursed God in their hearts." This was
Job's regular custom.

JOB 1:5 NIV

David pleaded with God for the child. He fasted and went into his house and spent the nights lying on the ground.

2 SAMUEL 12:16 NIV

BLESSING YOUR ENEMIES

▦ "But I tell you who hear me: Love your enemies, do good to those who hate you, bless those who curse you, pray for those who mistreat you."

LUKE 6:27–28 NIV

▦ "But I say to you, love your enemies and pray for those who persecute you."

MATTHEW 5:44 NASB

▦ [Stephen] fell to his knees, shouting, "Lord, don't charge them with this sin!" And with that, he died.

ACTS 7:60 NLT

▦ Jesus said, "Father, forgive them, for they do not know what they are doing." And they divided up his clothes by casting lots.

LUKE 23:34 NIV

INTERCEDING FOR OTHERS

■ So we have not stopped praying for you since we first heard about you. We ask God to give you complete knowledge of his will and to give you spiritual wisdom and understanding.

COLOSSIANS 1:9 NLT

■ And this I pray, that your love may abound still more and more in real knowledge and all discernment, so that you may approve the things that are excellent, in order to be sincere and blameless until the day of Christ; having been filled with the fruit of righteousness which comes through Jesus Christ, to the glory and praise of God.

PHILIPPIANS 1:9–11 NASB

■ And I am praying that you will put into action the generosity that comes from your faith as you understand and experience all the good things we have in Christ.

PHILEMON 1:6 NLT

■ So we keep on praying for you, asking our God to enable you to live a life worthy of his call. May he give you the power to accomplish all the good things your faith prompts you to do. Then the name of our Lord Jesus will be honored because of the way you live, and you will be honored along with him. This is all made possible because of the grace of our God and Lord, Jesus Christ.

2 THESSALONIANS 1:11–12 NLT

■ And may the Lord make your love for one another and for all people grow and overflow, just as our love for you overflows. May he, as a result, make your hearts strong, blameless, and holy as you stand before God our Father when our Lord Jesus comes again with all his holy people. Amen.

1 THESSALONIANS 3:12–13 NLT

Therefore, confess your sins to one another, and pray for one another so that you may be healed. The effective prayer of a righteous man can accomplish much.

JAMES 5:16 NASB

LOOKING FOR
EVANGELISTIC
OPPORTUNITIES

■ He said to his disciples, "The harvest is great,
but the workers are few. So pray to the Lord
who is in charge of the harvest; ask him to
send more workers into his fields."

MATTHEW 9:37–38 NLT

■ Pray also for me, that whenever I open my
mouth, words may be given me so that I
will fearlessly make known the mystery of
the gospel, for which I am an ambassador in
chains. Pray that I may declare it fearlessly,
as I should.

EPHESIANS 6:19–20 NIV

■ For this I will praise you, O LORD, among the
nations, and sing to your name.

PSALM 18:49 ESV

Sing a new song to the LORD!
Let the whole earth sing to the LORD!
Sing to the LORD; praise his name.
Each day proclaim the good news
that he saves.
Publish his glorious deeds among the nations.
Tell everyone about the amazing things
he does.

PSALM 96:1–3 NLT

Then Jesus came to them and said, "All
authority in heaven and on earth has been
given to me. Therefore go and make disciples
of all nations, baptizing them in the name of
the Father and of the Son and of the Holy
Spirit, and teaching them to obey everything
I have commanded you. And surely I am with
you always, to the very end of the age."

MATTHEW 28:18–20 NIV

153

ONE MOMENT
AT A TIME

REMEMBERING
OTHERS

Don't let "out of sight, out of mind" happen to you. Hang a small bulletin board or build a small photo album of pictures of people you want to pray for regularly. Use these images as a reminder to keep those you love in prayer.

Don't become overwhelmed. When you add in relatives, friends, coworkers, and even enemies, you may generate a long list of people you hope to pray for. Rather than get overwhelmed because the list is so long, try dividing them up for days of the week. For example, on Monday pray for people from church; Tuesday pray for extended family; Wednesday pray for coworkers, and so forth.

Post prompters. Tape a note or two to different places you traffic each day as prompters to pray for the people listed on each one. Good places to tape notes may include your computer, bathroom mirror, or refrigerator.

CHAPTER 9

QUALITIES OF EFFECTIVE PRAYER

I was at the store last week and saw a perfect illustration of myself. I watched this young child being disruptive. He was both loud and out of control. When his mother tried to call him over to get his attention, the youngster defiantly looked at her, yelled "no," and kept acting out. I admit, my first thought was judgmental toward the mother. How could she let that child act that way? As I left the store and starting walking to my car I realized, Oh my goodness, that's me. How many times does God beckon me and I defiantly go my own way? How many times do I forget to treat Him with respect? More times than I can even remember.

■ Juanita, age 41, New York ■

PRIORITIZING PURITY

▣ The eyes of the Lord are on the righteous
and his ears are attentive to their cry.

PSALM 34:15 NIV

▣ "God blesses those whose hearts are pure,
for they will see God."

MATTHEW 5:8 NLT

▣ The Lord is far from the wicked,
but he hears the prayer of the righteous.

PROVERBS 15:29 ESV

▣ The end of all things is near. Therefore be
clear minded and self-controlled so that you
can pray.

1 PETER 4:7 NIV

▣ I want everyone everywhere to lift innocent
hands toward heaven and pray, without being
angry or arguing with each other.

1 TIMOTHY 2:8 CEV

■ Truly God is good to Israel,

> to those who are pure in heart.

But as for me, my feet had almost stumbled,

> my steps had nearly slipped.

For I was envious of the arrogant

> when I saw the prosperity of the wicked....

And they say, "How can God know?

> Is there knowledge in the Most High?"...

If I had said, "I will speak thus,"

> I would have betrayed the generation
> of your children....

Nevertheless, I am continually with you;

> you hold my right hand....

Whom have I in heaven but you?

And there is nothing on earth that I desire

> besides you.

My flesh and my heart may fail,

> but God is the strength of my heart and
> my portion forever.

PSALM 73:1–26 ESV

■ But know that the LORD has set apart the
　　godly man for Himself;
The LORD hears when I call to Him.

PSALM 4:3 NASB

■ LORD, I call to you; come quickly to me. Hear
my voice when I call to you. . . . Set a guard
over my mouth, O LORD; keep watch over
the door of my lips.

PSALM 141:1, 3 NIV

KEEPING THE FAITH

■ "You can pray for anything, and if you have faith, you will receive it."

MATTHEW 21:22 NLT

■ "If you abide in me, and my words abide in you, ask whatever you wish, and it will be done for you."

JOHN 15:7 ESV

■ I lift up my eyes to the hills—
where does my help come from?
My help comes from the LORD,
the Maker of heaven and earth.

PSALM 121:1–2 NIV

■ And without faith it is impossible to please Him, for he who comes to God must believe that He is and that He is a rewarder of those who seek Him.

HEBREWS 11:6 NASB

O my people, trust in him at all times.
Pour out your heart to him, for God is our
refuge.

PSALM 62:8 NLT

Let us draw near to God with a sincere
heart in full assurance of faith, having our
hearts sprinkled to cleanse us from a guilty
conscience and having our bodies washed
with pure water.

HEBREWS 10:22 NIV

In him and through faith in him we may
approach God with freedom and confidence.

EPHESIANS 3:12 NIV

DEPENDING ON THE HOLY SPIRIT

And pray in the Spirit on all occasions with all kinds of prayers and requests. With this in mind, be alert and always keep on praying for all the saints.

EPHESIANS 6:18 NIV

In the same way, the Spirit helps us in our weakness. We do not know what we ought to pray for, but the Spirit himself intercedes for us with groans that words cannot express. And he who searches our hearts knows the mind of the Spirit, because the Spirit intercedes for the saints in accordance with God's will.

ROMANS 8:26–27 NIV

And because you are sons, God has sent the Spirit of his Son into our hearts, crying, "Abba! Father!"

GALATIANS 4:6 ESV

QUIETING YOURSELF

■ "Be still, and know that I am God!
I will be honored by every nation.
I will be honored throughout the world."

PSALM 46:10 NLT

■ Be still before the LORD and wait patiently
for him; fret not yourself over the one who
prospers in his way, over the man who
carries out evil devices!

PSALM 37:7 ESV

■ He makes me lie down in green pastures,
he leads me beside quiet waters,
he restores my soul.
He guides me in paths of righteousness
for his name's sake.

PSALM 23:2–3 NIV

I remember the days of old;
I meditate on all Your doings;
I muse on the work of Your hands.

PSALM 143:5 NASB

So what shall I do? I will pray with my spirit,
but I will also pray with my mind; I will sing
with my spirit, but I will also sing with my
mind.

1 CORINTHIANS 14:15 NIV

They will speak of the glorious splendor of
your majesty, and I will meditate on your
wonderful works.

PSALM 145:5 NIV

Instead, I have calmed and quieted myself,
like a weaned child who no longer
cries for its mother's milk.
Yes, like a weaned child is my soul within me.

PSALM 131:2 NLT

BEING PERSISTENT

■ Seek the LORD and His strength;
  Seek His face continually.

> 1 CHRONICLES 16:11 NASB

■ Let us hold tightly without wavering to the hope we affirm, for God can be trusted to keep his promise.

> HEBREWS 10:23 NLT

■ I praise you seven times a day because your laws are fair.

> PSALM 119:164 CEV

■ You paid attention to me, and so I will pray to you as long as I live.

> PSALM 116:2 CEV

■ Then, teaching them more about prayer, he used this story: "Suppose you went to a friend's house at midnight, wanting to borrow three loaves of bread. You say to him, 'A friend of mine has just arrived for a visit, and I have nothing for him to eat.' And suppose he calls out from his bedroom, 'Don't bother me. The door is locked for the night, and my family and I are all in bed. I can't help you.' But I tell you this—though he won't do it for friendship's sake, if you keep knocking long enough, he will get up and give you whatever you need because of your shameless persistence.

"And so I tell you, keep on asking, and you will receive what you ask for. Keep on seeking, and you will find. Keep on knocking, and the door will be opened to you."

LUKE 11:5–9 NLT

167

Then Jesus told his disciples a parable to show them that they should always pray and not give up. He said: "In a certain town there was a judge who neither feared God nor cared about men. And there was a widow in that town who kept coming to him with the plea, 'Grant me justice against my adversary.'

"For some time he refused. But finally he said to himself, 'Even though I don't fear God or care about men, yet because this widow keeps bothering me, I will see that she gets justice, so that she won't eventually wear me out with her coming!' "

And the Lord said, "Listen to what the unjust judge says. And will not God bring about justice for his chosen ones, who cry out to him day and night? Will he keep putting them off? I tell you, he will see that they get justice, and quickly. However, when the Son of Man comes, will he find faith on the earth?"

LUKE 18:1–8 NIV

Be joyful in hope, patient in affliction, faithful in prayer.

ROMANS 12:12 NIV

Pray without ceasing.

1 THESSALONIANS 5:17 KJV

FINDING TIME IN THE MORNING AND EVENING

■ By day the Lord commands his steadfast love, and at night his song is with me, a prayer to the God of my life.

PSALM 42:8 ESV

■ But I call to God, and the Lord saves me. Evening, morning and noon I cry out in distress, and he hears my voice.

PSALM 55:16–17 NIV

■ Lord, the God who saves me, day and night I cry out before you. . . .
But I cry to you for help, O Lord; in the morning my prayer comes before you.

PSALM 88:1, 13 NIV

■ Accept my prayer as incense offered to you, and my upraised hands as an evening offering.

PSALM 141:2 NLT

■ Give ear to my words, O LORD;
    consider my groaning....
Lord, in the morning you hear my voice;
    in the morning I prepare a sacrifice for
    you and watch.

PSALM 5:1, 3 ESV

■ Before daybreak the next morning, Jesus got
up and went out to an isolated place to pray.

MARK 1:35 NLT

■ I rise early, before the sun is up;
    I cry out for help and put my hope
    in your words.
I stay awake through the night,
    thinking about your promise.

PSALM 119:147–148 NLT

171

HUMBLING YOUR HEART

If my people, who are called by my name, will humble themselves and pray and seek my face and turn from their wicked ways, then will I hear from heaven and will forgive their sin and will heal their land.

2 CHRONICLES 7:14 NIV

Good and upright is the LORD;
therefore he instructs sinners in the way.
He leads the humble in what is right,
and teaches the humble his way.

PSALM 25:8–9 ESV

Since God chose you to be the holy people he loves, you must clothe yourselves with tenderhearted mercy, kindness, humility, gentleness, and patience.

COLOSSIANS 3:12 NLT

Humble yourselves, therefore, under God's mighty hand, that he may lift you up in due time. Cast all your anxiety on him because he cares for you.

1 PETER 5:6–7 NIV

ONE MOMENT
AT A TIME
STAYING
FOCUSED

■ **Try praying with ACTS.** Demonstrated in the organization of this book, the ACTS model of prayer can help organize your prayer time. Divide your prayer time into four sections, taking appropriate amounts of time for prayers of Adoration (or praise), prayers of Confession, prayers of Thanksgiving, and prayers of Supplication (or asking for God's help).

■ **Go for a walk.** Go for a walk and enjoy nature. Look for objects along the way that can remind you of God's character. For example, a small rock might remind you of God's strength. A leaf might remind you of the

life He provides. Pick up one or two of them
and carry them along as reminders of God's
character while you pray.

Create a bookmark. Choose a verse from
this chapter that has been the best reminder
to you about offering effective prayer. Create
a bookmark you place in your Bible or prayer
journal and begin to memorize the verse as
you pray this next week.

CHAPTER 10

HINDRANCES TO PRAYER

As a pastor, one of the biggest complaints I hear from my congregation is that they feel like their prayers are "bouncing off the ceiling." To many, God often seems distant and their prayers seem to go unheard. Sometimes we go through natural seasons where our emotions cause us to feel that way. Other times, though, there's a specific reason we feel distant: It's because we are distant. We have put up our own ceiling of pride, doubts, fears, anxiety, or sin. When those things happen, we become the cause of our own problem.

■ Melvin, age 63, Illinois ■

HAVING ANXIETY AND DOUBT

Don't worry about anything; instead, pray about everything. Tell God what you need, and thank him for all he has done.

PHILIPPIANS 4:6 NLT

If any of you lacks wisdom, he should ask God, who gives generously to all without finding fault, and it will be given to him. But when he asks, he must believe and not doubt, because he who doubts is like a wave of the sea, blown and tossed by the wind. That man should not think he will receive anything from the Lord.

JAMES 1:5–7 NIV

■ "If God gives such attention to the appearance of wildflowers—most of which are never even seen—don't you think he'll attend to you, take pride in you, do his best for you? What I'm trying to do here is to get you to relax, to not be so preoccupied with *getting*, so you can respond to God's *giving*. People who don't know God and the way he works fuss over these things, but you know both God and how he works. Steep your life in God-reality, God-initiative, God-provisions. Don't worry about missing out. You'll find all your everyday human concerns will be met.

"Give your entire attention to what God is doing right now, and don't get worked up about what may or may not happen tomorrow. God will help you deal with whatever hard things come up when the time comes."

MATTHEW 6:30–34 MSG

BEING FILLED WITH HYPOCRISY OR PRIDE

■ "And when you pray, do not be like the hypocrites, for they love to pray standing in the synagogues and on the street corners to be seen by men. I tell you the truth, they have received their reward in full."

MATTHEW 6:5 NIV

■ There are six or seven kinds of people the LORD doesn't like: Those who are too proud or tell lies or murder, those who make evil plans or are quick to do wrong, those who tell lies in court or stir up trouble in a family.

PROVERBS 6:16–19 CEV

■ The LORD is more pleased when we do what is right and just than when we offer him sacrifices.

Haughty eyes, a proud heart, and evil actions are all sin.

PROVERBS 21:3–4 NLT

He also told this parable to some who trusted in themselves that they were righteous, and treated others with contempt: "Two men went up into the temple to pray, one a Pharisee and the other a tax collector. The Pharisee, standing by himself, prayed thus: 'God, I thank you that I am not like other men, extortioners, unjust, adulterers, or even like this tax collector. I fast twice a week; I give tithes of all that I get.' But the tax collector, standing far off, would not even lift up his eyes to heaven, but beat his breast, saying, 'God, be merciful to me, a sinner!' I tell you, this man went down to his house justified, rather than the other. For everyone who exalts himself will be humbled, but the one who humbles himself will be exalted."

LUKE 18:9–14 ESV

HOLDING ON TO SELFISHNESS AND SIN

■ The LORD detests the sacrifice of the wicked, but he delights in the prayers of the upright.

PROVERBS 15:8 NLT

■ If I had not confessed the sin in my heart, the Lord would not have listened.

PSALM 66:18 NLT

■ "We know that God does not hear sinners; but if anyone is God-fearing and does His will, He hears him."

JOHN 9:31 NASB

■ My God will reject them because they have not obeyed him; they will be wanderers among the nations.

HOSEA 9:17 NIV

■ You ask and do not receive, because you ask with wrong motives, so that you may spend it on your pleasures.

JAMES 4:3 NASB

■ If you won't help the poor,
   don't expect to be heard when you cry out for help.

PROVERBS 21:13 CEV

■ "And when you stand praying, if you hold anything against anyone, forgive him, so that your Father in heaven may forgive you your sins."

MARK 11:25 NIV

ONE MOMENT
AT A TIME

BREAKING
THROUGH

Pray out loud. If you normally pray silently,
try going to a private place and speaking your
prayer out loud. Talk to God as you would
talk to a friend. Whether you pray silently or
with your lips, God will hear you.

Pray a psalm. The psalms are some of the
most powerful prayers in the Bible and a helpful way to stimulate your own prayer. If you
need a psalm of praise, try reading Psalms 19,
47, 66, 100, 103, or 104. If you need a psalm
of confession, try Psalm 51. For thanksgiving,
turn to Psalm 136. Dealing with doubts? Read
Psalms 13 and 73. And if anxiety weighs you
down, read Psalms 1, 23, 46, and 139.

Read a book on prayer. A book on the subject of prayer can be a great way to deepen your prayer life. Books worth considering: *Prayer* by Richard Foster; *Too Busy Not to Pray* by Bill Hybels; *Becoming a Woman of Prayer* by Cynthia Heald; *Letters to Malcom Chiefly on Prayer* by C. S. Lewis; *The Practice of the Presence of God* by Brother Lawrence; and *Prayer* by Ole Hallesby.

CONCLUSION

Three things have helped me improve my
intimacy with God. First, I set aside daily time to
pray. Sometimes I can afford a full hour, sometimes it's a lot shorter—but I try never to miss
my appointment with God. Second, I don't let my
morning "Amen" cut off my conversation with
God. Since God is always with me, I talk to Him
believing that He is alongside me every day.
I thank Him for good things, pray for people
as we encounter them, and ask for His help
when challenges arrive. Third, I read my Bible.
The Bible helps me understand God better
and lets me hear from Him. While in prayer I do
most of the talking, by reading the Bible I get
to do most of the listening.

■ Walter, age 30, British Columbia ■

FINDING INTIMACY WITH GOD

■ Yes. What other great nation has gods that are intimate with them the way GOD, our God, is with us, always ready to listen to us?

DEUTERONOMY 4:7 MSG

■ "Here I am! I stand at the door and knock. If you hear my voice and open the door, I will come in and eat with you, and you will eat with me."

REVELATION 3:20 NCV

■ The LORD your God will always be at your side, and he will never abandon you.

DEUTERONOMY 31:6 CEV

■ We saw it, we heard it, and now we're telling you so you can experience it along with us, this experience of communion with the Father and his Son, Jesus Christ.

1 JOHN 1:3 MSG

Then Jesus declared, "I am the bread of life. He who comes to me will never go hungry, and he who believes in me will never be thirsty."

JOHN 6:35 NIV

"Live in me. Make your home in me just as I do in you. In the same way that a branch can't bear grapes by itself but only by being joined to the vine, you can't bear fruit unless you are joined with me."

JOHN 15:4 MSG

God is faithful, by whom you were called into the fellowship of his Son, Jesus Christ our Lord.

1 CORINTHIANS 1:9 ESV

ONE MOMENT
AT A TIME

GOING DEEPER

■ **Build a memorial.** Often in Old Testament stories, the people of Israel set up a memorial to remind themselves what God had done. Consider building one of your own. Put a jar on your dresser and place a small rock inside the jar every time you see God answer a prayer. (You might even consider writing the answer on the rock.) Over time, as the jar fills up, you'll be encouraged to see how God interacts with your life.

■ **Plant something.** Plant a tree or shrub in your yard (or a flower indoors) that reminds you of God's beauty and care in your life. Tend to the plant regularly just as you tend to your prayer life. And while you do your part in nurturing it, you'll enjoy seeing God make it grow.

Encourage someone else along the way.
Having a prayer partner can be a practical way for you (and that person) to grow in faith. E-mail and text each other requests and praise and then meet periodically to pray together.

Look for all the
What the Bible Says About...
books from Barbour Publishing

What the Bible Says about
GOD'S WILL
ISBN 978-1-60260-279-3

What the Bible Says about
EMOTIONS
ISBN 978-1-60260-281-6

What the Bible Says about
WORSHIP
ISBN 978-1-60260-280-9

192 pages / 3 ¾" × 6" / $4.97 each

Available wherever Christian books are sold.